DATE DUE

MAR 1 7 2016 JUL 0 6 2016		
JUL 3 0 2016		
SEP 1 5 2016		
OCT 2 9 2016		
NOV 1 4 2016		
MAY 3 0 2017		
		PRINTED IN U.S.A.

GREAT AMERICAN HUMOR

1000 Funny Jokes, Clever One-Liners & Witty Sayings

Gerd de Ley

Great American Humor

Text Copyright © 2015 Gerd de Ley

Library of Congress Cataloging-in-Publication Data is available.

ISBN: 978-1-57826-609-8

Interior Design by Carolyn Kasper

Printed in the United States

10 9 8 7 6 5 4 3 2 1

CONTENTS

INTRODUCTION

FOR DECADES I've been collecting and translating original quotations and aphorisms in many languages. Of the more than 100,000 English language quotations I've collected, I've always preferred the very witty ones. And, in my collection, the witty Americans comprise the majority of these humorous sentiments.

To make a compilation of the very best American quips and quotes was inevitable, and here they are: some 1,000 funny—yet often wise—one-liners of famous (and not-so-famous) American writers, actors, comedians, politicians, and what I call "occasional aphorists."

I hope the reader will enjoy this collection as much as I enjoyed putting it together.

—Gerd de Ley

— ★ —

LIFE, LIBERTY
AND THE
PURSUIT
OF LAUGHTER

— ★ —

Free advice is worth the price.
　　—ROBERT HALF

Advice is given freely because so much of it is worthless.
　　—JAMES GEARY

You simply *must* stop taking advice from other people.
　　—MELISSA TIMBERMAN

My grandfather's a little forgetful, but he likes to give me advice. One day, he took me aside and left me there.
　　—RON RICHARDS

For sincere personal advice and the correct time, phone any number at random at 3 A.M.
　　—STEVE MARTIN

Never say "oops" in the operating room.
>—LEO TROY

Never say "never" and always avoid "always."
>—JOHN M. HAZLITT

Don't wear fur. Did you know that a single fur coat takes 14 trees just for the protest signs?
>—EMO PHILIPS

Never change diapers in midstream.
>—DON MARQUIS

Never get deeply in debt to someone who cried at the end of *Scarface*.
>—ROBERT S. WIEDER

Never get into S&M with a guy who wears imitation leather.
>—JOAN RIVERS

Never kick a fresh turd on a hot day.
　　　—HARRY S. TRUMAN

Never watch anything stupider than you.
　　　—BETTE MIDLER

Never play poker with a man called Ace.
　　　—LINDSEY NELSON

Never insult a police officer while he's doing a body cavity search.
　　　—FRASER MCCLURE

Never wear any latex or rubber undergarment except for recreational purposes.
　　　—JOAN RIVERS

Never shake hands with a man holding a chainsaw.
　　　—WILLIAM BROADERSEN

Never sit on a barbwire fence naked.
—Texas Bix Bender

Never approach a friend's girlfriend or wife with mischief as your goal. There are too many women in the world to justify that sort of dishonorable behavior. Unless she's really attractive.
—Bruce Jay Friedman

Never pick your nose when you're working with superglue.
—Emo Philips

Never let your mind write a check your body can't cash.
—Lewis Grizzard

Never hire an electrician whose eyebrows are scorched.
—Mason Wilder

Never tell a woman that you didn't realize she was pregnant unless you're certain that she is.
—DAVE BARRY

Never sleep with a fat man in July.
—MODINE GUNCH

Never try to tell everything you know. It may take too short a time.
—NORMAN FORD

Never try to adjust your clothing in a crowded elevator.
—WILLIAM BROADERSEN

Never undress in front of a bearded lady.
—EVAN ESAR

Never trust a naked bus driver.
—JACK DOUGLAS

Never trust a man who combs his hair straight from his left armpit.

—ALICE ROOSEVELT LONGWORTH

Never approach a bull from the front, a horse from the rear or a fool from any direction.

—KEN ALSTAD

Never answer an anonymous letter.

—YOGI BERRA

Never give your boy all the allowance you can afford. Keep some in reserve to bail him out.

—JOSH BILLINGS

Never moon a werewolf.

—MIKE BINDER

Never kiss the hand of a lady after she's been to the self-service gas station.

—WILLIAM BROADERSEN

Never let a fool kiss you, or a kiss fool you.
>—JOEY ADAMS

Never impute criminal intent where stupidity will suffice.
>—LAWRENCE DAVID

Never attribute to malice what can be adequately explained by stupidity.
>—NICK DIAMOS

Never, ever go to bed with a man on the first date. Not ever. Unless you really want to.
>—CYNTHIA HEIMEL

Never sneeze while leaning your head against a brick wall.
>—JOHN MORRISON RAYMOND, III

Always take time to stop and smell the roses, and sooner or later, you'll inhale a bee.
>—TERRY MARCHAL

Always shop for nothing; you'll always come back with something.

—LISA MENDOZA

Always try to keep a smile on your face because it looks silly on other parts of your body.

—GENE PERRET

Men, always aim high. That way you won't splash on your shoes.

—MILTON BERLE

Always walk tall and keep your head up—unless you're walkin' in a cow pasture.

—TEXAS BIX BENDER

Always look out for number one—and be careful not to step in number two.

—RODNEY DANGERFIELD

Always refrain from inserting a finger into an uncertain hole.

—LEA DELARIA

Always tell her she is beautiful, especially if she is not.

—ROBERT A. HEINLEIN

It is always wise to tip well on the way up in case you meet the same greedy cunts on the way down.

—P.V. TAYLOR

When checking for gas leaks, always remember to use *safety matches* to prevent accidents.

—LAWRENCE BROTHERTON

Remember there's a big difference between kneeling down and bending over.

—FRANK ZAPPA

Remember, if you can get along with one woman, you can get along with more.

—ARTHUR BAER

Just remember: it's lonely at the top, when there's no one on the bottom.

> —RODNEY DANGERFIELD

Remember compliments you receive. Forget the insults.

If you succeed in doing this, tell me how.

> —KURT VONNEGUT

Always remember that wearing less will get you more.

> —JOAN RIVERS

Don't point that beard at me, it might go off.

> —ROBERT PIROSH, GEORGE SEATON,
> AND GEORGE OPPENHEIMER

Don't try to step into a revolving door behind someone and expect to come out ahead.

> —JOSEPH CHARLES SALAK

Don't talk about yourself; it will be done when you leave.

—ADDISON MIZNER

Rule 1: Don't panic.
Rule 2: Panic first.

—WALTER RUSSELL MEAD

Don't ever make the same mistake twice, unless it pays.

—MAE WEST

Don't forget to tell everyone it's a secret.

—GERALD F. LIEBERMAN

Don't meet trouble halfway. It is quite capable of making the entire journey.

—BOB EDWARDS

Don't worry if you're a kleptomaniac, you can always take something for it.

—ROBERT BENCHLEY

Don't do it if you can't keep it up.

—JOHNNY CARSON

Don't look in the mirror and say, "I love you."
The mirror is most likely to reply, "Couldn't
we just be friends?"

—LEA DELARIA

Don't ever send a man window shopping. He'll
come back carrying a window.

—DIANA JORDAN
AND PAUL SEABURN

Don't gamble; take all your savings and buy
some good stock and hold it till it goes up,
then sell it. If it don't go up, don't buy it.

—WILL ROGERS

Please don't talk while I am interrupting.

—TODD ROCKEFELLER

The best way to keep your friends is not to give them away.

—WILSON MIZNER

The best way to behave is to misbehave.

—MAE WEST

The best way to confuse a drummer is to put a sheet of music in front of him.

—LIZZY DAVENPORT

The best way to cure a pain in the behind is to kiss 'em goodbye.

—TEXAS BIX BENDER
AND GLADIOLA MONTANA

The best way to remember your wife's birthday is to forget it once.

—ELI JOSEPH COSSMAN

The best way to get your tomatoes to ripen is to go on holiday. The tomatoes will sense your absence, ripen, rot and fall to the ground before you get back—even if you are gone for only two days.

—FRED KELLER

The best way to get great ideas is to get lots of ideas and throw the bad ones away.

—CHARLES "CHIC" THOMPSON

The best way to make a fire with two sticks is to make sure one of them is a match.

—WILL ROGERS

The easiest way to change history is to become a historian.

—PAUL DICKSON

The easiest way to find something lost around the house is to buy a replacement.

—JACK ROSENBAUM

The easiest way to diminish the appearance of wrinkles is to keep your glasses off when you look in the mirror.

—JOAN RIVERS

The only way to combat criminals is by not voting for them.

—DAYTON ALLEN

The only way to get over someone is to get under someone else.

—KERRY COHEN

When in doubt, use brute force.

—KEN THOMPSON

When in doubt, sing loud.

—ROBERT MERRILL

When in doubt, remain in doubt.

—JAMES GEARY

When you are dissatisfied and would like to go back to youth, think of algebra.

—GENE YASENAK

When you have nothing to say, sing it.

—DAVID OGILVY

When everyone else zigs, zag.

—TOM YOBAGGY

When authorities warn you of the sinfulness of sex, there is an important lesson to be learned. Do not have sex with the authorities.

—MATT GROENING

For others who may not know this: when the preacher says, "You may now kiss the bride," he's only speaking to the groom.

—DAVID GUNTER

When all else fails, read the instructions.

—AGNES ALLEN

When a man steals your wife, there is no better revenge than to let him keep her.
—DAVID BISSONETTE

When your IQ rises to 28, sell.
—IRWIN COREY

When you don't know what to do, walk fast and look worried.
—BOB DUCKLES

When government offers you something for free, run.
—STEVE KALAFER

When angry, count to four; when very angry, swear.
—MARK TWAIN

If everything else fails, throw it away.
—JIM MURRAY

If all else fails, immortality can always be assured by spectacular error.

—J.K. Galbraith

If at first you don't succeed, you must be doing something wrong.

—Charles Merrill Smith

If at first you don't succeed, destroy all evidence that you tried.

—Susan Ohanian

If at first you don't succeed, well, so much for skydiving.

—Victor O'Reilly

If she looks young—she's old. If she looks old—she's young. If she looks back...follow her.

—Gerald F. Lieberman

If thine enemy offend thee, give his child a drum.

—FRAN LEBOWITZ

If you have to ask if somebody is male or female, don't.

—PATRICK MURRAY

If you talk in your sleep, only date people with the same name.

—CRAIG SMITH

If you think nobody cares if you're alive, try missing a couple of car payments.

—EARL WILSON

If you go back in time, be careful not to step in anything.

—MATT GROENING

Tip: If a customs officer asks for your visa, don't say, "I have cash. Do you take that?"
—SCOTT ADAMS

If you're going to kill yourself with an axe, get it right the first time.
—SUZANNE MARTIN

If he asks, "Your place or mine?" say, "Both. You go to your place and I'll go to mine."
—BETTE MIDLER

If you want to be safe on the streets at night, carry a projector and slides of your last vacation.
—HELEN MUNDIS

If you're going to America, bring your own food.
—FRAN LEBOWITZ

If you don't think women are explosive, drop one.

—GERALD F. LIEBERMAN

If you want to find out some things about yourself—and in vivid detail too—just try calling your wife fat.

—P.J. O'ROURKE

If you wait long enough, suddenly nothing will happen.

—JACK GARDNER

If you go flying back through time, and you see somebody else flying forward into the future, it's probably best to avoid eye contact.

—JACK HANDY

If you're yearning for the good old days, just turn off the air conditioning.

—GRIFF NIBLACK

If you use a waffle iron for a pillow, be sure it is unplugged.

—GARY OWENS

If he says you're too good for him, believe it.

—DEBBIE PARSON

If you need to know directions, ask a man with one leg...If there's a shortcut, he knows where it is.

—DAVE ATTELL

If you want to recapture your youth, just cut off his allowance.

—AL BERNSTEIN

Sincerity is everything. If you can fake that, you've got it made.

—GEORGE BURNS

Beware the naked man who takes out his wallet.

—JASON CURABIA

Better to do nothing
Than waste time.

—ERIC NELSON

It is better to light just one candle than to clean the whole apartment.

—EILEEN COURTNEY

It is better to copulate than never.

—ROBERT A. HEINLEIN

Financial advice:
Making a million dollars is the simplest thing in the world. Just find a product that sells for $2000 and that you can buy at a cost of $1000, and sell a thousand of them.

—JERRY GILLIES

The safest way to double your money is to fold it over once and put it in your pocket.

—KIN HUBBARD

There is a very easy way to return from a casino with a small fortune: Go there with a large one.

—JACK YELTON

Your chances of winnin' the lottery get a lot better if you buy a ticket.

—WINSTON GROOM

Buy land. They've stopped making it.

—MARK TWAIN

Buy thermometers in the wintertime. They're much lower then.

—SOUPY SALES

Never wave to your friends at an auction.

—WILLIAM BROADERSEN

Never use a ten-dollar bill as a torch to find nickels in the snow.

—LEO HELZEL

Never invest in anything that eats or needs repainting.

—BILLY ROSE

Always buy sheep and sell deer.

—TIM WHITAKER

Don't spend $2 to dry-clean a shirt. Donate it to the Salvation Army instead. They'll clean it and put it on a hanger.

Next morning buy it back for 75 cents.

—BILLIAM CORONEL

Be careful not to do your good deeds when there's no one watching you.

—TOM LEHRER

Be obscure clearly.

—E.B. WHITE

There's one way to find out if a man is honest—ask him. If he says "yes," you know he is crooked.

—GROUCHO MARX

Madness takes its toll; please have exact change ready.

—STEVEN WRIGHT

There are several good precautions against temptation, but the surest is cowardice.

—MARK TWAIN

Lead us not into temptation. Just tell us where it is; we'll find it.

—SAM LEVENSON

It's easier to pray for forgiveness than to resist temptation.

—SOL KENDON

Where lipstick is concerned, the important thing is not the color, but to accept God's final decision on where your lips end.

—JERRY SEINFELD

Say the best.
Think the rest.

—CRAIG SEIBOLD

Date a homeless woman. It's easier to talk her into staying over.

—GARRY SHANDLING

Use the last key in the bunch because that's the only one that will unlock the door.

—CHARLES J. MUETH

The way to make a film is to begin with an earthquake and work up to a climax.

—CECIL B. DeMILLE

In any organization, there will always be one person who knows what is going on. This person must be fired.

—COLIN J. WYNNE

To really annoy people, shout random numbers when somebody is counting something.

—MIKE McQUEEN

You should place a woman on a pedestal, high enough so you can look up her dress.

—STEVE MARTIN

"Be yourself" is about the worst advice you can give to some people.

—TOM MASSON

Thou shalt not covet thy neighbor's house unless they have a well-stocked bar.

—W.C. FIELDS

Work is the greatest thing in the world, so we should always save some of it for tomorrow.
—DON HEROLD

It's so simple to be wise. Just think of something stupid to say and say the opposite.
—SAM LEVENSON

Here's a good rule of thumb:
Too clever is dumb.
—OGDEN NASH

"You haven't got the guts to pull that trigger" is almost always a bad thing to say.
—RUSSELL BELL

You can trust a crystal ball about as far as you can throw it.
—FAITH POPCORN

Advice for poker players:
Look around the table. If you don't see a sucker, get up, because you're the sucker.
> —THOMAS AUSTIN PRESTON JR.
> (AKA AMARILLO SLIM)

You've got to have smelled a lot of mule manure before you can sing like a hillbilly.
> —HANK WILLIAMS

You gotta get up early in the morning to catch a fox, and stay up late at night to get a mink.
> —MAE WEST

To sell something, tell a woman it's a bargain; tell a man it's deductible.
> —EARL WILSON

Want to have some fun? Walk into an antique shop and say, 'What's new?'
> —HENNY YOUNGMAN

Make sure you're not at the airport when your ship comes in.
—JASON LOVE

Look over your shoulder now and then to be sure someone's following you.
—HENRY GILMER

A good time to keep your mouth shut is when you're in deep water.
—SIDNEY GOFF

Getting out of jury duty is easy. The trick is to say you're prejudiced against all races.
—MATT GROENING

Living in a vacuum sucks.
—ADRIENNE E. GUSOFF

You don't learn from smart people, you learn from idiots. Watch what they do, and then don't do it.

—MINNESOTA FATS

Thou shall not commit adultery...unless in the mood.

—W.C. FIELDS

Sometimes the best you can do is move the turd to another pocket.

—SCOTT ADAMS

Accept that some days you're the pigeon and some days you're the statue.

—ROGER ANDERSEN

Love your enemy—it will scare the hell out of him.

—ALEX AYRES

You can stop almost everything from functioning by hitting it with a large rock.

—RUSSELL BELL

The only good reason to leave a party without thanking the host and hostess is if you weren't invited.

—TEXAS BIX BENDER

Here is a useful shopping tip: you can get a pair of shoes for one pound at bowling alleys.

—AL CLETHEN

The best time to debate with family members is when they have food in their mouths.

—KENNETH COLE

Get your cut throat off my knife.

—DIANE DI PRIMA

My advice is: Keep the vibrator and recycle the man.

—BETTY DODSON

It's okay to laugh in the bedroom so long as you don't point.
—WILL DURST

Laughing at our mistakes can lengthen our own life. Laughing at someone else's can shorten it.
—CULLEN HIGHTOWER

Dyslexics of the world, untie!
—ANDREW JAMNER

In painting a ceiling, a good rule of thumb is that there should be at least as much paint on the ceiling as on your hair.
—P.J. O'ROURKE

It is important to keep an open mind, but not so open that your brains fall out.
—STEPHEN A. KALLIS, JR.

It doesn't matter what anybody tells you.
Now shut up and listen!
—WILLIAM KENNEDY

You need a mobile phone. How else can you let
people know that you are on the train?
—ROB MOSELEY

There are very few personal problems that
cannot be solved through a suitable applica-
tion of high explosives.
—SCOTT ADAMS

— ★ —

WE HOLD THESE LAUGHS TO BE SELF-EVIDENT

— ★ —

The trouble with facts is that there are so many of them.

—SAMUEL MCCHORD CROTHERS

Let's face facts, shall we? There is a very real possibility that this could also be the *last* day of the rest of your life.

—DAVE HENRY

Boomerang users have many happy returns.

—LINDA WILLIAMS

One reassuring thing about modern art is that things can't be as bad as they are painted.

—M. WALTHALL JACKSON

It is difficult to see why lace should be so expensive; it is mostly holes.

—MARY WILSON LITTLE

Every good journalist has a novel in him—
which is an excellent place for it.
—RUSSELL LYNES

A study of economics usually reveals that the
best time to buy anything was last year.
—MARTY ALLEN

The trouble with born-again Christians is
that they are a bigger pain the second time
around.
—HERB CAEN

A lot of people never use their initiative because nobody ever tells them to.
—MARY ALLEN

Forecasting is very difficult, especially if it's
about the future.
—EDGAR R. FIEDLER

Unfortunately, this world is full of people who are ready to think the worst when they see a man sneaking out of the wrong bedroom in the middle of the night.

—WILL CUPPY

Change is good. Particularly when you've been wearing the same underwear for several days.

—MATT DIAMOND

If you can't seem to find your glasses, it's probably because you don't have them on.

—DELORES DRAKENBERG

Reading the epitaphs, our only salvation lies in resurrecting the dead and burying the living.

—PAUL ELDRIDGE

In some families, the problems are relative.

—SAM EWING

We all have to die someday, if we live long enough.
>   —DAVE FARBER

The report of my death was an exaggeration.
>   —MARK TWAIN

If you hang yourself, you die of your own free will and accord.
>   —HENNY YOUNGMAN

The only thing wrong with immortality is that it tends to go on forever.
>   —HERB CAEN

One can't be immortal after one dies.
>   —DAVID MAMET

Saying "I'm sorry" is the same as saying "I apologize." Except at a funeral.
>   —DEMETRI MARTIN

If you don't go to other men's funerals, they won't go to yours.

—CLARENCE DAY

If you expect nothing, you're apt to be surprised. You'll get it.

—MALCOLM S. FORBES

When working toward the solution of a problem it always helps if you know the answer.

—JOHN PEERS

Any simple problem can be made unsolvable if enough meetings are held to discuss it.

—MARK TWAIN

No problem is so big or so complicated that it can't be run away from.

—CHARLES SCHULZ

When the only tool you have is a hammer, every problem begins to look like a nail.

> —ABRAHAM MASLOW

Whenever I reflect upon the events of the summer of 1776, I feel thankful that I wasn't one of the Founding Fathers. Because I'd be dead now.

> —DAVID GUNTER

When someone hands you a flier it's like they're saying, "Here, you throw this away."

> —MITCH HEDBERG

A poet who reads his own verse in public may have other nasty habits.

> —ROBERT A. HEINLEIN

Summer Help. And some are not.

> —R.F. HEISEY

There are two kinds of directors in the theater. Those who think they are God and those who are certain of it.

—RHETTA HUGHES

It's one of the tragic ironies of the theatre that only one man in it can count on steady work—the night watchman.

—TALLULAH BANKHEAD

Many a standing ovation has been caused by someone jumping to his feet in an effort to beat the rest of the audience to the parking lot.

—EARL WILSON

Modesty in an actor is as fake as passion in a call girl.

—JACKIE GLEASON

An actor with too much money will usually find a way to get rid of it.

—AL PACINO

If a farmer fills his barn with grain, he gets mice; if he leaves it empty, he gets actors.

—BILL VAUGHAN

Movie stars and monogamy go together like cornflakes and Tabasco.

—JULIA LLEWELLYN SMITH

If it weren't for the Japanese and Germans, we wouldn't have any good war movies.

—STANLEY RALPH ROSS

The trouble with jogging is that by the time you realize you're not in shape for it, it's too far to walk back.

—FRANKLIN P. JONES

Nothing in the world can replace the modern swimsuit, and it practically has.

—KIRK KIRKPATRICK

Now I know why they call those bathing suits Bikinis. They don't cover the girls atoll.

—ROBERT ORBEN

The nice thing about being a celebrity is that when you bore people, they think it's their fault.

—HENRY KISSINGER

If fools could fly, this place would be a major airport.

—BERT WEIS

The only time a bachelor's bed is made is when it is in the factory.

—P.J. O'ROURKE

Somebody figured it out—we have 35 million laws trying to enforce Ten Commandments.

—EARL WILSON

In this country you're guilty until proven wealthy.
—BILL MAHER

Irrigation of the land with seawater desalinated by fusion power is ancient. It's called rain.
—MICHAEL MCCLARY

Rain is caused by high-pressure areas; cold fronts; warm, moist air; and weekends.
—PAUL SWEENEY

When somebody says, "The last thing I want to do is hurt you," it means that they've got other things to do first.
—MARK SCHIFF

They are not really fixing the streets. They are just moving the holes around so the motorists cannot memorize them.
—HERB SHRINER

What's more enchanting than the voices of young people, when you can't hear what they say?

—LOGAN PEARSALL SMITH

If you find a plumber that is free, there must be a reason.

—LESLIE LYLES

You know you've really made it when your toupee blows off at the office and no one dares to laugh.

—FRANK RIDGEWAY

No one heard him laugh like that since his wife died.

—LEO ROSTEN

There are two kinds of adhesive tape—that which won't stay on and that which won't come off.

—MARIA TELESCO

There are two different kinds of people in this world: those who finish what they start, and

—BRAD RAMSEY

Things are not as bad as they seem. They are worse.

—BILL PRESS

Artificial insemination is nothing compared to the real thing.

—JOAN RIVERS

The mind is much more powerful than the prick—and the mind doesn't go down in two minutes.

—ROBIN TYLER

The reason lightning doesn't strike twice in the same place is that the same place isn't there the second time.

—WILLIE TYLER

There are exceptions to every rule, except this one.

—FRANK L. VISCO

What if everything is an illusion and nothing exists? In that case, I definitely overpaid for my carpet.

—WOODY ALLEN

I've found it's easier to remember your mother's wedding date if you were actually there at the ceremony.

—RICK LIPPINCOTT

The one thing you will never find in a teenager's bedroom is the floor.

—BRUCE LANSKY

People are more violently opposed to fur than leather, because it's safer to pick on rich women than biker gangs.

—LENNY SCHAFER

Although the moon is only one-sixth the size of the Earth, it's much further away.
—PAT BAILEY

A day without sunshine is like night.
—STEVE MARTIN

God put the waterworks too close to the playground.
—LEE SCHREINER

If it wasn't for half the people in the world, the other half would be all of them.
—COL. LEMUEL STOOPNAGLE

It is difficult to keep quiet if you have nothing to say.
—MALCOLM MARGOLIN

The concept behind the mobile phone is that you have absolutely nothing to say and you've got to talk to someone about it right now.

    —JERRY SEINFELD

Cordless phones are great. If you can find them.

    —GLENN FOSTER

Misers are no fun to live with, but they make great ancestors.

    —TOM SNYDER

When you don't know what you're talking about, it's hard to know when you're finished.

    —TOMMY SMOTHERS

Well, I think I'll call it a day—because after all, that's what it is.

    —TOM SIMS

There are two types of dirt: the dark kind, which is attracted to light objects, and the light kind, which is attracted to dark objects.

—ELY SLICK

All men can fly, but sadly only in one direction —down.

—SYDNEY J. HARRIS

Only the nose knows,
Where the nose goes,
When the door close.

—MUHAMMAD ALI

Conscience doesn't stop you from doing what you shouldn't, it just stops you from enjoying it.

—CLEVELAND AMORY

If your nose runs and your feet smell, you're put together backwards.

—STEVE MARTIN

You know, the good thing about gangs is they carpool.

—JOHN MENDOZA

If you don't know where you are going, you might wind up someplace else.

—YOGI BERRA

Wherever you go...there you are.

—EARL MAC RAUCH

Anywhere is walking distance, if you've got the time.

—STEVEN WRIGHT

A great many open minds should be closed for repairs.

—TOLEDO BLADE

If you are not confused, you have not been paying attention.

—DAVE MCNEELY

When two pessimists meet they shake heads instead of hands.

—HUNTER MADSEN

Everything is still the same. It's just a little different now.

—GEORGE CARLIN

If some people said what they thought, they'd be speechless.

—MARSHA COLEMAN

All modern men are descended from a worm-like creature, but it shows more on some people.

—WILL CUPPY

Mountain climbers rope themselves together to prevent the sensible ones from going home.

—EARL WILSON

A perfect summer day is when the sun is shining, the breeze is blowing, the birds are singing, and the lawnmower is broken.

—JAMES DENT

It's a sure sign of summer if the chair gets up when you do.

—WALTER WINCHELL

A lot of fellows nowadays have a B.A., M.D., or Ph.D.
Unfortunately, they don't have a J.O.B.

—FATS DOMINO

If other people are going to talk, conversation becomes impossible.

—JAMES MCNEILL WHISTLER

The trouble with modern apartments is: The walls are too thin when you try to sleep, and too thick when you try to listen!

—HARVEY KURTZMAN

What's right is what's left if you do everything else wrong.
> —SYMAN HIRSCH

A signature always reveals a man's character—and sometimes even his name.
> —EVAN ESAR

Only a light bulb can go out every night and still be bright the next day!
> —HARVEY KURTZMAN

Nothing makes you more tolerant of a neighbor's noisy party than being there.
> —FRANKLIN P. JONES

A neighbor will stand at your door talking for 20 minutes because she doesn't have time to come in
> —SAM EWING

For every complex natural phenomenon there is a simple, elegant, compelling, wrong explanation.

> —THOMAS GOLD

The advantage of a classical education is that it enables you to despise the wealth which it prevents you from achieving.

> —RUSSELL GREEN

Being frustrated is disagreeable, but the real disasters of life begin when you get what you want.

> —IRVING KRISTOL

If hard work were such a wonderful thing, surely the rich would have kept it all to themselves.

> —LANE KIRKLAND

Unemployment is not working.

> —SYMAN HIRSCH

Twenty percent of zero is better than nothing.
>—Walt Kelly

Few persons invent algebra on their own.
>—Frederick Mosteller

Five out of four people have trouble with fractions.
>—Steven Wright

Counting in octal is just like counting in decimal—if you don't use your thumbs.
>—Tom Lehrer

If you can keep your head when all about you are losing theirs, it's just possible you haven't grasped the situation.
>—Jean Kerr

Everyone has a right to be stupid. Some just abuse the privilege.
>—James T. Hammond

The only reason some people get lost in thought is because it's unfamiliar territory.

—PAUL FOX

Most transvestites are just regular guys, who occasionally like to eat, drink and be Mary.

—JOE JOSEPH

Let smile be your umbrella, and you'll get a lot of rain in your face.

—GARY RABINOWITZ

The man who smiles when things go wrong has thought of someone to blame it on.

—THOMAS F. JONES, JR.

Let's be honest: Isn't a lot of what we call tap-dancing really just nerves?

—JACK HANDY

If you could understand Morse code, a tap-dancer would drive you crazy.

—MITCH HEDBERG

People in the seventh century before Christ had no idea they were living in the seventh century B.C.

—Joseph Heller

It is more fun contemplating somebody else's navel than your own.

—Arthur Hoppe

When people don't want to come, nothing will stop them.

—Sol Hurok

If there was no capital punishment, there'd be no Easter.

—Bill Hicks

Sticking feathers up your butt does not make you a chicken.

—Chuck Palahniuk

The longest word in the English language is the one that follows the phrase, "And now a word from our sponsor."

—HAL EATON

The two most beautiful words in the English language are "check enclosed."

—DOROTHY PARKER

Anyone who can only think of one way to spell a word obviously lacks imagination.

—MARK TWAIN

People who live in glass houses have to answer the bell.

—BRUCE PATTERSON

Nowadays, people can be divided into three classes—the Haves, the Have-Nots, and the Have-Not-Paid-for-What-They-Haves.

—EARL WILSON

The sum of intelligence on the planet is a constant; the population is growing.
　　　—HARRI V. TARANTO

He's a distinguished man of letters. He works for the Post Office.
　　　—MAX KAUFFMAN

The universe is a big place, perhaps the biggest.
　　　—KILGORE TROUT

Midgets are the last to know it's raining.
　　　—LARRY TUCKER

Eternal nothingness is fine if you happen to be dressed for it.
　　　—WOODY ALLEN

Today's public figures can no longer write their own speeches or books, and there is some evidence that they can't read them either.
　　　—GORE VIDAL

Nothing cures a case of homesickness like going home.

—UNCLE JOHN

The only thing that has to be finished by next Tuesday is next Monday.

—JENNIFER YANE

If you are what you do, and then you don't, you aren't.

—ROBERT SUBBY

Anyone who lives within his means suffers from a lack of imagination.

—LIONEL STANDER

You won't smell it until you step in it.

—BERNARD SPRING

If you lost your left arm, your right arm would be left.

—BREE SCHULTZ

When you've seen one pterodactyl you've seen them all.

—EDWARD WELLEN

Some people are so far behind in a race that they actually believe they are leading.

—FRANK RENZULLI

If something's old and you're trying to sell it, it's obsolete; if you're trying to buy it, it's a collector's item.

—FRANK ROSS

The only thing that can be guaranteed to stop falling hair is the floor.

—WILL ROGERS

If nature had intended our skeletons to be visible it would have put them on the outside of our bodies.

—ELMER RICE

Nothing is impossible for the man who doesn't have to do it himself.

—A.H. WEILER

People have one thing in common: they are all different.

—ROBERT ZEND

Everybody talks about the weather, but nobody does anything about it.

—CHARLES DUDLEY WARNER

What's right is what's left if you do everything else wrong.

—ROBIN WILLIAMS

The most predictable thing about the stock market is the number of experts who take credit for predicting it.

—DAVE WEINBAUM

Thanks to the invention of the telescope, planets that are 100 billion miles away look to be only 50 billion miles away.

—JOHN M. WAGNER

A knowledge of Sanskrit is of little use to a man trapped in a sewer.

—TOM WELLER

About the only time losing is more fun than winning is when you're fighting temptation.

—TOM WILSON

Those who flee temptation generally leave a forwarding address.

—LANE OLINGHOUSE

Resisting temptation is easier when you think you'll probably get another chance later on.

—BOB TALBERT

When you are down and out, something always turns up—and it is usually the noses of your friends.

—ORSON WELLES

There ought to be a better way of starting the day than having to get up.

—EARL WILSON

Say what you want about long dresses, but they cover a multitude of shins.

—MAE WEST

On the other hand, you have different fingers.

—STEVEN WRIGHT

The person who says "I won't say another word" always does.

—SUZAN L. WIENER

When there is a choice of two evils, most men take both.

—AUSTIN O'MALLEY

If you keep your mind sufficiently open, people will throw a lot of rubbish into it.
>—WILLIAM A. ORTON

All religions are the same: basically guilt, with different holidays.
>—CATHY LADMAN

Those who think they know it all are especially annoying to those of us who do.
>—HAROLD COFFIN

The quietest place in the world is the complaints department at the parachute packing plant.
>—JACKIE MARTLING

Nothing is really lost. It's just where it doesn't belong.
>—SUZANNE MUELLER

If you are sure you understand everything that is going on, you are hopelessly confused.
>—WALTER F. MONDALE

The only thing that works in an old house is the owner.
>—SPERO MCCONNELL

A compass is narrow-minded—it always points north
>—BILLY GRAHAM

It's not the bullet that kills you; it's the hole.
>—LAURIE ANDERSON

But why do I need a gun license?
It's only for use around the house.
>—CHARLES ADDAMS

If you water it and it dies, it's a plant. If you pull it out and it grows back, it's a weed
>—LEO GALLAGHER

Three may keep a secret if two of them are
dead.
—BENJAMIN FRANKLIN

Every maybe has a wife called maybe not.
—EARL DERR BIGGERS

If it is bright and sunny after two cold and
rainy days, it is probably Monday.
—HUGH B. BROUS JR.

The bridges you cross before you come to them
are over rivers that aren't there.
—GENE BROWN

The only person who listens to both sides of an
argument is the fellow in the next flat.
—RUTH BROWN

The most remarkable thing about pollsters is
how they find so many people with no opinion.
—DOUG LARSON

The trouble with telling a good story is that it invariably reminds the other fellow of a bad one.

—SID CAESAR

It's not the time it takes to take the take that takes the time; it's the time between the takes that takes the time to take the take.

—MARVIN CHOMSKY

Creativity is great, but plagiarism is faster.

—FREDERICK A. CLAY

The rat race isn't so bad if you're a big cheese.

—RAYMOND J. CVIKOTA

The biggest lie in life used to be "The check is in the mail." Now it's "Push here to open."

—GERALD DUNN

The shortcoming of some house guests is their long-staying.

—SAM EWING

Wall Street indices predicted nine out of the last five recessions!

—PAUL A. SAMUELSON

96.37% of all statistics are made up.

—KEVIN D. QUITT

My mom always complains about my lack of a boyfriend. Well, next time she asks, I'm going to tell her I'm dating two different guys: Mr. Duracell and Mr. Energizer.

—MICHELLE LANDRY

Really good magicians always leave church with a little more money than they came in with.

—ANDY PIERSON

If the Titanic had been a soap opera it'd still be sinking.

—ROBERT ORBEN

The reason people blame things on previous generations is that there's only one other choice.
—Doug Larson

Without electricity we would still be in the dark ages.
—Richard Lederer

A hole is nothing at all, but you can break your neck in it.
—Austin O'Malley

The sooner you make your first 5,000 mistakes, the sooner you will be able to correct them.
—Kimon Nicolaides

The worst thing about having a mistress is those two dinners you have to eat.
—Oscar Levant

The miniskirt enables young ladies to run faster, and because of it, they may have to.
— JOHN V. LINDSAY

The problem with bald guys is that you don't know where their face ends.
— JASON LOVE

A bit of talcum
Is always walcum.
— OGDEN NASH

If brains were dynamite you couldn't blow your nose.
— GEORGE LUCAS

I've noticed there are a lot of people named Rice, but no one seems to be named Corn.
— GEORGE CARLIN

To some the opposite of monotony is polygamy.
— GENE MORA

If opposites attracted, the North Pole and the South Pole would be married and living happily at the equator.

—GENE PERRET

On ships they call them barnacles; in business they call them vice-presidents.

—FRED ALLEN

Who needs astrology?
The wise man gets by on fortune cookies.

—EDWARD ABBEY

Base 8 is just like base 10, if you are missing two fingers.

—TOM LEHRER

THE LAWS OF LAUGHTER

Night watchmen in horror movies have a life expectancy of 12 seconds.

—SAM WAAS

When everything is coming your way, you're in the wrong lane.

—STEVEN WRIGHT

$100 invested at 7% interest for 100 years will become $100,000, at which time it will be worth absolutely nothing.

—ROBERT A. HEINLEIN

If it works right the first time, you've obviously done something wrong.

—PAT JETT

Not one man in a beer commercial has a beer belly.

—RITA RUDNER

Electric clocks reveal to you
Precisely when your fuses blew.
—LEONARD SCHIFF

Electric clocks aren't entirely useless when
the power goes off. They tell you exactly when
it happened.
—JANE GOODSELL

The guy you beat out of a prime parking space
is the one you have to see for a job interview.
—CAL ROBINSON

The duration of a modern marriage is in
direct proportion to the distance from one's
relatives.
—ROGER ROSENBLATT

Law of government: The amount of time
required to finish any project is equal to the
amount of time already spent on it.
—JAY TRACHMAN

The future, according to some scientists, will be exactly like the past, only far more expensive.

—JOHN SLADEK

There are two kinds of people, those who finish what they start and so on...

—ROBERT BYRNE

There are two kinds of people in the world: those who believe there are two kinds of people in the world and those who don't.

—ROSS F. PAPPRILL

There are two kinds of people entitled to refer to themselves as "we." One is an editor, the other is a fellow with a tapeworm.

—BILL NYE

I don't buy temporary insanity as a murder defense. Temporary insanity is breaking into someone's home and ironing all their clothes.

—SUE KOLINSKY

Juries scare me. I don't want to put my faith in 12 people who weren't smart enough to get out of jury duty.

—MONICA PIPER

The only difference between a cult and a religion is the amount of real estate they own.

—FRANK ZAPPA

If everything seems to be coming your way, you are probably in the wrong lane.

—MICHAEL MCDANIEL

Do you know the difference between education and experience?

Education is when you read the fine print; experience is what you get when you don't.

—PETE SEEGER

Most people don't know what they really want—but they're sure they haven't got it.

—ALFRED E. NEUMAN

The human brain starts working the moment you are born and never stops until you stand up to speak in public.

—GEORGE JESSEL

It takes a big man to cry, but it takes an even bigger man to laugh at that man.

—JACK HANDY

If it's free, it's advice; if you pay for it, it's counseling; if you can use either one, it's a miracle.

—JACK ADAMS

Just because you have an irrational fear of flying doesn't mean you're not going to crash.

—BOB REINSTEDT

As long as there is algebra there will be prayer in school.

—LARRY MILLER

If you don't like the way I drive, get off the sidewalk.

—LOTUS WEINSTOCK

Those who cannot remember the past will spend a lot of time looking for their cars in mall parking lots.

—JAY TRACHMAN

A pipe gives a wise man time to think and a fool something to stick in his mouth.

—ED TRISCHMANN

The laws of fishing:
1. The biggest fish always bite the smallest rod.
2. If two lines can get tangled, they will.
3. Whatever bait you're using, the fish are hitting something else.
4. As the hook is bent, so goes the fish.

—HERBERT C. QUOY

If it's there, you'll step in it.
If it's not, it's already on your shoe.
     —LARRY LINDVIG

Law of airlines: The shorter the time between flights, the greater the distance between gates.
     —DOUG LARSON

The first piece of luggage on the carousel belongs to no one. It's just a dummy suitcase to give everyone hope.
     —ERMA BOMBECK

Murphy's law of mountain bike navigation: The way you must go is always uphill.
     —CRAIG SMITH

No matter what direction you bike in, you will always have the wind in your face.
     —CRAIG SMITH

One ply toilet paper: If you can see through it, you can wee through it.

—STEPHANIE KOSCIELSKI

The more trees a developer cuts down, the woodsier the name of the resulting housing development.

—PAUL DICKSON

The writers of free verse got their idea from incorrect proof pages.

—ROBERT FROST

Astronomers point out that the universe is racing away from the Earth at 15,000 miles per second. Can you blame it?

—ALFRED E. NEUMAN

You can always get a job in international affairs because 90% of everything happens in a foreign country.

—STEVEN WRIGHT

When you are driving behind a slow-moving vehicle in a no-overtaking zone, that vehicle will always turn in the same direction at the same junction you do.

—JAMES DENT

The organization of any bureaucracy is very much like a septic tank—the really big chunks always rise to the top.

—JOHN IMHOFF

Any film with "bikini" in its title is a) going to show you some wobbly flesh, b) going to try to make you laugh and, c) fail.

—TIM HEALEY

If there is a 50-50 chance that something can go wrong, then nine times out of 10 it will.

—PAUL HARVEY

More boys would follow in their father's foot-steps if they weren't afraid of being caught.

—E.C. MCKENZIE

There are three kinds of researchers: Those who can do math and those who cannot.

—TOM RUSK VICKERY

A good musical comedy consists largely of disorderly conduct occasionally interrupted by talk.

—GEORGE ADE

A piano is a piano is a piano.

—GERTRUDE STEINWAY

There are a number of mechanical devices which increase sexual arousal, particularly in women. Chief among them is the Mercedes-Benz 380SL convertible.

—P.J. O'ROURKE

A cigarette is a much cheaper and more widely available alternative to nicotine patches.

—BOB DAVIES

Never take vacations
To visit relations.

 —GERALD BARZAN

A hotel is a place you give good dollars for bad quarters.

 —MARSHA COLEMAN

In every restaurant, the hardness of the butter increases in direct proportion to the softness of the bread.

 —RUDY JOE MANO

Law of software engineering: Don't worry if it doesn't work right. If everything did, you'd be out of a job.

 —CHARLES A. MOSHER

The probability of your knee hitting the leg of the table increases geometrically in direct relation to the amount of coffee in your cup.

 —BRUCE C. MCKINNEY

The laws of cartoon motion:

Any body suspended in space will remain in space until made aware of its situation.

Any body passing through solid matter will leave perforation conforming to its perimeter.

Any violent rearrangement of feline matter is impermanent.

A cat will assume the shape of its container.

—MARK O'DONNELL

The longer the description on the menu, the less you will get on your plate.

—SHIRLEY LOWE

Physics lesson: When a body is submerged in water, the phone rings.

—ERNIE LIMES

The amount of energy spent laughing at a joke should be directly proportional to the hierarchical status of the joke teller.

—SCOTT ADAMS

Any given company policy, rules, or procedure will outlast everybody's memory of why it was instituted.

—DON ADDIS

The badness of a movie is directly proportional to the number of helicopters in it.

—DAVE BARRY

Law of air travel: The strength of the turbulence is directly proportional to the temperature of the coffee.

—NICHOLAS GUNTER

The first pull on the cord will always send the drapes the wrong way.

—CHARLES P. BOYLE

The probability of a young man meeting a desirable and receptive young woman increases by pyramidical progression when he is already in the company of (1) a date, (2) his wife, (3) a better looking and richer male friend.

—RONALD H. BEIFELD

Telephones displace bodies immersed in water.

—MARTIN S. KOTTMEYER

A healthy adult male bore consumes each year one and a half times his own weight in other people's patience.

—JOHN UPDIKE

Any country with "democratic" in the title isn't.

—JIM MURRAY

Successful dieting is a triumph of mind over platter.

—GERALD F. LIEBERMAN

The toughest part of being on a diet is shutting up about it.

—GERALD NACHMAN

The second day of a diet is always easier than the first. By the second day you're off it.
—JACKIE GLEASON

Eating a pound of fattening foods puts more weight on than not eating it takes off.
—EDWIN MOISE

The average time between throwing something away and needing it badly is two weeks.
—NORMAN R. BELL

The amount of sleep the average person needs is about an hour more.
—SAM EWING

Basic rule for travel with kids:
Never in the same direction.
—WILLIAM E. GEIST

When preparing to travel, lay out all your clothes and money. Then take half the clothes and twice the money.

—SUSAN HELLER ANDERSON

Never take a cross-country trip with a kid who has just learned to whistle.

—JEAN DEUEL

The worst whistlers whistle the most.

—ROBERT E. MURRAY

There are only two laws:
Someday you will die.
If you read this, you are not dead yet.

—YVONNE G.T. DEVAULT

Life ain't easy. But then, if it was, everybody would be doing it.

—HARLAN ELLISON

Life is full of misery, loneliness, and suffer-ing—and it's all over much too soon.
> —WOODY ALLEN

Two great rules of life:
1. Never tell everything at once.
> —KEN VENTURI

Love is a word consisting of two vowels, two consonants, and two fools.
> —JEFF ROVIN

Love is the delightful interval between meet-ing a beautiful girl and discovering that she looks like a haddock.
> —JOHN BARRYMORE

WITH LAUGHS
AND WIT
FOR ALL

I went to the Missing Persons' Bureau. No one was there.

　　—GEORGE CARLIN

Most people are bothered by those passages of Scripture they do not understand, but the passages that bother me most are those I do understand.

　　—MARK TWAIN

I'm 42 around the chest, 52 around the waist, 92 around the golf course, and a nuisance around the house.

　　—GROUCHO MARX

I didn't attend the funeral, but I sent a nice letter saying I approved of it.

　　—MARK TWAIN

I have seen the future and it is just like the present, only longer.

—KEHLOG ALBRAN

Business is so bad in some cafés that waiters have to go out in the streets to insult people.

—FRED ALLEN

An actress I met assured me her real ambition was to be a waitress at a coffeehouse.

—WOODY ALLEN

My sister wanted to be an actress. She never made it, but she does live in a trailer... so she got halfway. She's an actress, she's just never called to the set.

—MITCH HEDBERG

Some movie stars wear their sunglasses even in church: They're afraid God might recognize them and ask for autographs.

—FRED ALLEN

I saw the sequel to the movie *Clones*, and you know what? It was the same movie.

—JIM SAMUELS

It has taken only 50 years for films to go from silent to unspeakable.

—DOUG LARSON

A trick I learned in show business is that if you sweat a lot in your clothes, they don't want them back.

—BILL MURRAY

I can't understand why a person will take a year to write a novel when he can easily buy one for a few dollars.

—FRED ALLEN

This must be a gift book. That is to say, a book which you wouldn't take on any other terms.

—DOROTHY PARKER

I went to a bookstore and asked the sales-woman, "Where's the self-help section?" She said if she told me, it would defeat the purpose.

—STEVEN WRIGHT

I do a lot of reading on serial killers: mostly *How To* books.

—ROSEANNE BARR

I've read some of your modern free verse and wonder who set it free.

—JOHN BARRYMORE

I was reading the dictionary. I thought it was a poem about everything.

—STEVEN WRIGHT

I don't think anyone should write their auto-biography until after they're dead.

—SAMUEL GOLDWYN

You know when you put a stick in water and it looks bent?
That's why I never take baths.

— STEVEN WRIGHT

Dear Junior:
Excuse me for not answering your letter sooner. I have been so busy not answering letters lately that I couldn't get around to not answering yours in time.

— GROUCHO MARX

Now that we have demonstrated that man can walk on the moon, it's time we proved he can walk down Main Street after dark.

— ROBERT FUOSS

Sometimes I think the surest sign that intelligent life exists elsewhere in the universe is that none of it has tried to contact us.

— BILL WATTERSON

A new study reveals that guests on daytime talk shows are predominantly female. Of course, most of them weren't born that way.

—CONAN O'BRIEN

I've got sticky tape on all the mirrors in my house so that I don't accidentally walk through into another dimension…

—STEVEN WRIGHT

We believe that electricity exists, because the electric company keeps sending us bills for it.

—DAVE BARRY

I bet there are little men in the walls that are in charge of the electrical outlets. I see one is on a smoke break right now.

—ANDY PIERSON

Cold! If the thermometer had been an inch longer we'd have all frozen to death!

—MARK TWAIN

Sometimes when I watch a parade, I wonder how many of the marchers are in desperate need of a good long piss.

—GEORGE CARLIN

Right-handers go over there, left-handers go over there, the rest of you, come with me.

—YOGI BERRA

I once built a ship in a bottle. They had to break the bottle to let me out.

—STEVEN WRIGHT

The weather is here. Wish you were beautiful.

—JIMMY BUFFETT

Weather forecast for tonight: Dark.

—GEORGE CARLIN

I've got a good mind to join a club and beat you over the head with it.

—GROUCHO MARX

If you can keep your head when all about you are losing theirs, you're probably the executioner.

—ELDEN CARNAHAN

My friend Larry's in jail now. He got 25 years for something he didn't do. He didn't run fast enough.

—DAMON WAYANS

I didn't recognize you without the handcuffs.

—JONATHAN LARSON

When I see the word "manslaughter," I like to think: "man's laughter," and then I don't feel so bad. Unfortunately, Grandpa was charged with aggravated homicide.

—BOB VAN VORIS

My brother-in-law wrote an unusual murder story. The victim got killed by a man from another book.

—ROBERT SYLVESTER

I went to the museum where they had all the heads and arms from the statues that are in all the other museums.

—STEVEN WRIGHT

If you're ashamed of being a wallflower, imagine how the wall feels.

—JACOB CHUROSH

I'd like to help the homeless but they're never home.

—LENNY CLARKE

To all my boyfriends—past, present, and future: I love you. I hate you. I miss you. I want my money back. Choose the one that applies to you.

—KIM COLES

A man committed suicide by overdosing on decongestant tablets. All they found was a pile of dust.

—STEVEN CONNELLY

This is the Suicide Hotline: please hold.

—RUBY WAX

A suicide hotline is where they talk to you until you don't feel like killing yourself. Exactly the opposite of telemarketing.

—DANA SNOW

We don't know who it was who discovered water, but we're pretty sure it wasn't a fish.

—FATHER JOHN CULKIN, S.J.

Neurotics build castles in the air, psychotics live in them. My mother cleans them.

—RITA RUDNER

Xerox sues somebody for copying?

—DAVID LETTERMAN

I xeroxed a mirror. Now I have an extra xerox machine.

—STEVEN WRIGHT

If you ever become a mother, can I have one of the puppies?

—CHARLES PIERCE

It's hard to lose a mother-in-law. In fact it's almost impossible.

—W.C. FIELDS

I told my mother-in-law that my house was her house, and she said, "Get the hell off my property."

—JOAN RIVERS

All those disorders. When I was a kid we just had crazy people.

—ELLEN DEGENERES

If I had a dollar for every time I've forgotten something, I don't know how much I'd have.

—STEVEN WRIGHT

I buried a lot of my ironing in the back yard.

—PHYLLIS DILLER

My new dress. Do you like it? It's from my favorite designer, On Sale.
—RITA RUDNER

Your right to wear a mint-green polyester leisure suit ends where it meets my eye.
—FRAN LEBOWITZ

The closest I came to a ménage à trois was once I dated a schizophrenic.
—RITA RUDNER

Nobody goes there anymore because it's always so crowded.
—YOGI BERRA

My old man always wanted me to be a garbage man. He thought they only worked on Thursdays.
—DENNIS HILL

They're a perfect match. He's a night watchman and she never worked a day in her life.

—SYMAN HIRSCH

My dad believes in reincarnation, so in his will he left everything to himself.

—BARRY GOLDSMITH

We had nothing to steal in our house. My uncle always said that if a burglar broke in he would leave a tip.

—JENNIFER PATTERSON

He was an angry man, Uncle Swanny. He had printed on his grave: "What are you lookin' at?"

—MARGARET SMITH

Last month, my aunt passed away. She was cremated. We think that's what did it.

—JONATHAN KATZ

If I held you any closer I would be on the other side of you.

  —GROUCHO MARX

These days, swimsuits are cut down to here or up to there. Most of them aren't suitable for women who have either no here or too much there.

  —MARY LINDLEY

I'm desperately trying to figure out why kamikaze pilots wore helmets.

  —DAVE HEDISON

He was a self-made man who owed his lack of success to nobody.

  —JOSEPH HELLER

The chance of forgetting something is directly proportional to... to...

  —LANE HUREWITZ

I went to a general store. They wouldn't let me buy anything specific.

  —STEVEN WRIGHT

You know when you step on a mat in the supermarket and the door opens? For years, I thought it was a coincidence.

  —RICHARD JENI

My son has taken up meditation—at least it's better than sitting doing nothing.

  —MAX KAUFFMANN

My sister gives me the creeps: all her old boyfriends.

  —TERRI KELLY

I'd give my right arm to be ambidextrous.

  —BRIAN W. KERNIGHAN

I'm tired of all this nonsense about beauty being only skin deep. That's deep enough. What do you want—an adorable pancreas?

—JEAN KERR

After all, what is your hosts' purpose in having a party? Surely not for you to enjoy yourself; if that were their sole purpose, they'd have simply sent champagne and women over to your place by taxi.

—P.J. O'ROURKE

My father is semi-retired. He goes halfway to work and then he comes home.

—TOMMY KOENIG

My father originated the limbo dance—trying to get into a pay toilet.

—SLAPPY WHITE

The tights on the male dancers were so tight you could see what religion they are.

—ROBIN WILLIAMS

Imagine if there were no hypothetical situations...

—JOHN MENDOZA

I hate housekeeping! You make the beds, do the dishes, dust, and six months later you have to start all over again.

—JOAN RIVERS

It is not an optical illusion; it just looks like one.

—PHIL WHITE

I'm looking for Miss Right, or at least Miss Right Now.

—ROBIN WILLIAMS

'Twixt the optimist and the pessimist
The difference is quite droll:
The optimist the doughnut sees,
The pessimist, the hole.

—MCLANDBURGH WILSON

I read about a preacher who said, "The greater the sinner, the greater the saint." I wish I had learned this years ago.

—ED PARRISH

I washed a sock. Then I put it in the dryer. When I took it out, it was gone.

—STEVEN WRIGHT

I wonder what the word for "dots" looks like in Braille.

—DEMETRI MARTIN

Family trees seem to produce a variety of nuts.

—E.C. MCKENZIE

You know your family is really stressed when conversations often begin with, "Put the gun down and then we can talk."

—MIKE MCQUEEN

I've been looking forward to this evening about as much as I'd look forward to having my prostate examined by the Incredible Hulk.

—JAN MURRAY

If this is to be the winter of our discontent, then I expect I'll need a new coat of some kind.

—HENRY MARTIN

Now is the winter of our discontent made glorious summer by central heating.

—JACK SHARKEY

Blessed are the flexible, for they will not be bent out of shape.

—MICHAEL MCGRIFFY

I forgot and left the lighthouse on all night. Next day the sun wouldn't rise.

—ROD SCHMIDT

I bought a house, on a one-way, dead-end road. I don't know how I got there.

—STEVEN WRIGHT

It is generally agreed that "Hello" is an appropriate greeting because if you entered a room and said "Goodbye," it could confuse a lot of people.

—DOLPH SHARP

My friend thought he was not gonna make it; then he started thinking positive. Now he's positive he's not gonna make it.

—BROTHER SAMMY SHORE

The ad in the paper said "Big Sale. Last Week!" Why advertise? I already missed it. They're just rubbing it in.

—YAKOV SMIRNOFF

Radio news is bearable. This is due to the fact that while the news is being broadcast, the disc jockey is not allowed to talk.

—FRAN LEBOWITZ

Some people think a juggler is talented. Could be a schizophrenic playing catch.

—BOB DUBAC

In 1909 the first magician appeared on stage. He was so bad, he made the audience disappear.

—DARYL STOUT

This either a forgery or a very clever original.

—FRANK SULLIVAN

The trouble with people who don't have much to say is that you have to listen so long to find out.

—ANN LANDERS

Before I speak, I have something important to say.

  —GROUCHO MARX

It's not hard to understand modern art. If it hangs on a wall it's a painting, and if you can walk around it, it's a sculpture.

  —SIMON UPDIKE

The fact that no one understands you doesn't mean you're an artist.

  —MACEDDIE

I figure you have the same chance of winning the lottery whether you play or not.

  —FRAN LEBOWITZ

I know that there are people who do not love their fellow man, and I hate people like that!

  —TOM LEHRER

I know the difference between sadist and masochist...but you're going to have to beat it out of me.

—SCOTT LEITER

They tell me he was so crooked that when he died they had to screw him into the ground.

—WALTER DE LEON AND LYNN STARLING

Black people have never rioted. A riot is what white people think blacks are involved in when they burn stores.

—JULIUS LESTER

The hands on my biological clock are giving me the finger.

—WENDY LIEBMAN

The trouble with Francine's biological clock is that there's no happy hour.

—BOB THAVES

I've actually seen a man walk up to four women sitting in a bar and say, "Hey, what are you doing all alone?"

—LILY TOMLIN

He'll regret it to his dying day—if he ever lives that long.

—FRANK S. NUGENT

Dwn wth vwls.

—RUTH OLLINS

Thanksgiving is so called because we are all so thankful that it only comes once a year.

—P.J. O'ROURKE

He and I had an office so tiny that an inch smaller and it would have been adultery.

—DOROTHY PARKER

I bet a lot of mimes choke to death because nobody believes they're really choking.

—JOHN GEPHART

There is so much apathy in the world today...
but who cares?

—STEVEN J. PAUL

All those who believe in telekinesis, raise my
hand.

—EMO PHILIPS

A Zen master once said to me "Do the opposite
of whatever I tell you." So I didn't.

—JAMES PIERCE

She does not understand the concept of Roman
numerals. She thought we just fought World
War Eleven.

—JOAN RIVERS

Yesterday I was walking down the street
wearing my eyeglasses when my prescription
ran out.

—STEVEN WRIGHT

The agony of having spilled acid down my pants was quickly tempered by the breathtaking, once-in-a-lifetime opportunity to watch a penis melt.

—MIKE RAMPTON

My friends and I always use fruit instead of chips when we play poker.

Last week I won with two pear.

—DANIEL REIHS

I stayed up all night playing poker with tarot cards.

I got a full house and four people died.

—STEVEN WRIGHT

The first time I see a jogger smiling, I'll consider it.

—JOAN RIVERS

We use 10 percent of our brains. Imagine how much we could accomplish if we used the other 60.

—ELLEN DEGENERES

A Merry Christmas to all my friends except two.

—W.C. FIELDS

My husband is so cheap. On Christmas Eve he fires one shot and tells the kids Santa committed suicide.

—PHYLLIS DILLER

Meretricious and a Happy New Year.

—GORE VIDAL

Get real stoned: Drink wet cement.

—BREE SCHULTZ

During job interviews, when they ask, "What is your worst quality?," I always say, "Flatulence." That way I get my own office.

—DAN THOMPSON

We were so poor when I was growing up, if we wanted a Jacuzzi, we had to fart in the tub.
—EDDIE MURPHY

Flying—hours and hours of boredom sprinkled with a few seconds of sheer terror.
—GREGORY "PAPPY" BOYINGTON

Don't fly on any airline where the pilots believe in reincarnation.
—SPALDING GRAY

You know the oxygen masks on airplanes? I don't think there's really any oxygen. I think they're just to muffle the screams.
—RITA RUDNER

Never say "Hi Jack" in an airport.
—TERRY DENTON

Jews and Arabs should settle their differences like good Christians.

—WARREN R. AUSTIN

I was raised in the Jewish tradition, taught never to marry a Gentile woman, shave on Saturday and, most especially, never to shave a Gentile woman on Saturday.

—WOODY ALLEN

One of the oldest problems puzzled over in the Talmud is: "Why did God create goyim?" The generally accepted answer is "Somebody has to buy retail."

—ARTHUR NAIMAN

My best friend is a guy half Italian, half Jewish. If he can't buy it wholesale, he steals it.

—JACKIE MASON

Life is the ever dwindling period between abortion and euthanasia.

    —PATRICK MURRAY

I like life. It's something to do.

    —RONNIE SHAKES

I do not believe in an afterlife, although I am bringing a change of underwear.

    —WOODY ALLEN

Lif is too short.

    —BART GOLD

Love is the only game that will never be postponed on account of rain.

    —HOMER HAYNES

A lot of people wonder how you know if you're really in love. Just ask yourself this one question: "Would I mind being destroyed financially by this person?"

    —RONNIE SHAKES

The music teacher came twice each week to bridge the awful gap between Dorothy and Chopin.

—GEORGE ADE

He's my favorite kind of musician. He knows how to play the ukulele, but he doesn't.

—WILL ROGERS

I worry that the person who thought up musak may be thinking up something else.

—JANE WAGNER

All music is folk music. I ain't never heard no horse sing a song.

—LOUIS ARMSTRONG

If music be the breakfast of love, kindly do not disturb until lunch-time.

—JAMES AGEE

Karaoke bars combine two of nation's greatest evils: people who shouldn't drink with people who shouldn't sing.

—TOM DREESEN

Global warming? When my globes get warm, I just take off my sweater.

—DOLLY PARTON

Save the whales. Collect the whole set.

—STEVEN WRIGHT

Over 90 percent of high school students think BC means Before Cable.

—ARGUS HAMILTON

The only thing that ever kept me from going to college was high school.

—EDWARD FRIEDMAN

I was thrown out of college for cheating—with the dean's wife.

— WOODY ALLEN

Sex should not be taught in schools, unless the teacher really wants to learn.

— MORTY GUNTY

They're a perfect match. She's a mathematics teacher and he's a guy with a lot of problems.

— SYMAN HIRSCH

My niece was in *The Glass Menagerie* at school. They used Tupperware.

— CATHY LADMAN

I think a secure profession for young people is history teacher, because in the future, there will be so much more of it to teach.

— BILL MUSE

"You've waltzed with me enough," said my dancing teacher. "Now it's time you stood on your own feet."

—ALAN LEWIS

I got an A in philosophy because I proved that my professor didn't exist.

—JUDY TENUTA

It's good sportsmanship not to pick up lost balls while they are still rolling.

—MARK TWAIN

I used to compete in sports, and then I realized: You can buy trophies. Now I'm good at everything.

—DEMETRI MARTIN

The reason women don't play football is that 11 of them would never wear the same outfit in public.

—PHYLLIS DILLER

Nobody in the game of football should be called a genius. A genius is somebody like Norman Einstein.

—JOE THEISMANN

Basketball…is staying in after school in your underwear.

—RING LARDNER

Cricket is basically baseball on valium.

—ROBIN WILLIAMS

Hockey is a sport for white men. Basketball is a sport for black men. Golf is a sport for white men dressed like black pimps.

—TIGER WOODS

Golf is a game in which you yell "fore," shoot six and put down five.

—PAUL HARVEY

Last week I missed a spectacular hole-in-one by only five strokes.

—Bob Hope

Give me my golf clubs, fresh air, and a beautiful girl, and you can keep my golf clubs and the fresh air.

—Jack Benny

Hockey is a game where you take a stick and hit either the puck, or anyone who has touched the puck.

—Gene Perret

My brother-in-law died. He was a karate expert, then he joined the army. The first time he saluted, he killed himself.

—Henny Youngman

Sport of skiing—wearing 3,000 dollars' worth of clothes and equipment and driving for 200 miles in the snow in order to stand around a bar and get drunk.

—P.J. O'Rourke

I say, why pay outrageous prices for ski trips when I can just stick my face in the freezer and fall down on the kitchen floor.

—JOHN M. WAGNER

Cross-country skiing is great if you live in a small country.

—STEVEN WRIGHT

Swimming isn't a sport. It's just a way to keep from drowning.

—GEORGE CARLIN

Television is a device that permits people who haven't anything to do watch people who can't do anything.

—FRED ALLEN

Television remote control—the most effective birth-control device in history.

—JAY LENO

I wish there was a knob on the TV to turn up the intelligence. There's a knob called brightness, but it doesn't work.

—EUGENE B. GALLAGHER

On cable TV they have a weather channel—24 hours of weather. We had something like that where I grew up. We called it a window.

—DAN SPENCER

I once saw a one-armed juggler juggling three tennis balls at a carnival. Later, on TV, I saw an old Ed Sullivan Show where a guy was juggling three swords. I wonder if it was that same guy.

—STEVEN SUGG

A husband would rather turn the television on than his wife.

—CY DEBOER

I admit the most recent fight with my wife was my fault. She said, "What's on the TV?" and I said: "Dust."

—ROY BROWN

Traffic was so heavy it was bumper to bumper. A man pushed a cigarette lighter in, and the woman in the car in front said, "Ouch!"

—HENNY YOUNGMAN

I told the traffic warden to go forth and multiply, though not exactly in those words.

—WOODY ALLEN

In many cases the most dangerous part of a car is the nut that holds the steering wheel.

—JOE MOORE

My car doesn't have a manual because it's an automatic.

—STEVEN WRIGHT

From where she parked the car it was just a short walk to the footpath.

    —WOODY ALLEN

To my wife, double parking means on top of another car.

    —DAVE BARRY

One time I went to a drive-in in a taxi cab. The movie cost me $95.

    —STEVEN WRIGHT

Who would give me a driver's license? I got two tickets on my written test.

    —PHYLLIS DILLER

If we don't change direction soon, we'll end up where we're going.

    —IRWIN COREY

...and always remember the last words of my grandfather, who said "A truck!"

    —EMO PHILIPS

No phone pole ever hit a truck unless it was in self-defense.
> —JAMES CURTIS

The leading cause of death among fashion models is falling through street grates.
> —DAVE BARRY

I asked the sales assistant in the clothing store if she had anything to make me look thinner, and she said, "How about a week in Ethiopia?"
> —ROSEANNE BARR

A recent police study found that you're much more likely to get shot by a fat cop if you run.
> —DENNIS MILLER

Reducing diet—the taming of the chew.
> —SHELLY FRIEDMAN

It's not the minutes we spent at the table that put on weight. It's the seconds.

—SAM EWING

Little snax
Bigger slax.

—RUTH S. SCHENLEY

I'm on a seafood diet—I see food, I eat it.

—DOLLY PARTON

Who is General Failure and why is he reading my hard disk?

—STEVEN WRIGHT

Trudst me: doint evEr usee yoiur conpuitwer as a jellok miold.

—JOHN GEPHART

Beware of programmers who carry screwdrivers.

—LEONARD BRANDWEIN

I asked my son if he understood the meaning of the word "obey." He said, "Yeah, it's a place to go shopping on the Internet."

—JAY TRACHMAN

I still remember a time when having a web site meant it was time to dust.

—RICHARD M. ROMANO

The doctor told me to stop smoking. The doctor added, "And since you're quitting—I'll give you five dollars for your gold lighter."

—PAUL LYNDE

My neighbor asked me for a cigarette. I said, "I thought you'd stopped smoking." He said, "Well, I've managed the first stage—I've stopped buying them."

—JOEY ADAMS

Nicotine patches are great. Stick one over each eye and you can't find your fags.

—BILL HICKS

Those nicotine patches seem to work pretty well, but I understand it's hard to keep 'em lit.

—GEORGE CARLIN

They say if you smoke you knock off 10 years. But it's the last 10. What do you miss? The drooling years?

—JOHN MENDOZA

The only thing that bothers me is if I'm in a restaurant and I'm eating and someone says, "Hey, mind if I smoke?" I always say, "No. Mind if I fart?"

—STEVE MARTIN

You know what bugs me? People who smoke cigars in restaurants. That's why I always carry a water pistol filled with gasoline.

—PAUL PROVENZA

Remember, if you smoke after sex you're doing it too fast.

—WOODY ALLEN

I think passive smoking is outrageous. They should buy their own.

—JENNY ABRAMS

If you look like your passport photo, you're probably too ill to travel.

—WILL KOMMEN

If people looked like their passport photos, very few nations would let them in.

—DOUG LARSON

When I feel like getting away from it all, I just turn the TV on to a Spanish soap opera and imagine I'm on vacation in a hotel in Mexico.

—BRIAN MCKIM

I booked a flight the other day and the clerk asked, "How many people will be traveling with you?" I said, "I don't know. It's your plane."

—STEVEN WRIGHT

The scientific theory I like best is that the rings of Saturn are composed entirely of lost airline luggage.

—MARK RUSSELL

A man walks into a hotel and asks, "Do you take children?" The clerk replies, "No, only cash or MasterCard."

—BREE SCHULTZ

My wife was unable to obtain a hotel room with a bidet. I suggested that she do a handstand in the shower.

—BILLY WILDER

What a hotel: The towels were so big and fluffy, you could hardly close your suitcase.

—HENNY YOUNGMAN

A hotel mini-bar allows you to see into the future at what a can of Pepsi will cost in 2020.

—RICH HALL

"Room service? Send up a larger room."
—GROUCHO MARX

The last motel I stayed at had a two-speed air conditioner—loud and deafening.
—JOHN M. WAGNER

CONGRATULATIONS AND HAPPY BIRTHDAY ON YOUR ANNIVERSARY THIS VALENTINE'S DAY, BAR MITZVAH BOY, HOPE YOU FEEL BETTER SOON.
—ED BRODSKY

Hello, I must be going.
—GROUCHO MARX

LAUGHTER
AND THE
AMERICAN
LEXICON

A

aardvark: alphabetically advantaged animal.
—WILLIAM FLIS

abstract art: a product of the untalented, sold by the unprincipled to the utterly bewildered.
—AL CAPP

advertising: the art of convincing people to spend money they don't have on something they don't need.
—WILL ROGERS

advertising man: yessir, nosir, ulcer.
—ROBERT MYERS

alibi: to be able to prove you were somewhere else when you committed the crime.
—JIMMY DURANTE

alone: in bad company.
—AMBROSE BIERCE

ambivalence: watching your mother-in-law drive over a cliff in your new Cadillac.
—DAVID MAMET

anorexia: another word for nothing left to lose.
—JOY BEHAR

aria: Italian for "a song that will not end in your lifetime."
—DAVE BARRY

arthritis: twinges in the hinges.
—G.B. HOWARD

ashtray: something for a cigarette butt when there is no floor.
—ROBERT MYERS

atom bomb: an explosive device under which all people are cremated equal.
—JOEL ROTHMAN

B

bachelor: a thing of beauty and a boy forever.
—HELEN ROWLAND

bachelorhood: one way of keeping all that alimony money for yourself.
—GENE PERRET

bagpipes: the missing link between music and noise.
—E.K. KRUGER

baldness: nudism on a higher level.
—FRANK SINATRA

balloon: bad breath holder.
—DEMETRI MARTIN

bankruptcy: a legal proceeding in which you put your money in your pants pocket and give your coat to your creditors.
—JOEY ADAMS

beer baron: a malty millionaire.
—ROBERT MYERS

bikers: living proof that you can wear leather and not look sexy.
—JOHN M. WAGNER

born executive: a guy whose father owns the business.
—HARVEY KURTZMAN

buffet: a French term. It means get up and get it yourself.

    —GREG RAY

builder's estimate: a sum of money equal to half the final cost.

    —NEIL COLLINS

business: the art of extracting money from another man's pocket without resorting to violence.

    —MAX AMSTERDAM

C

caddie: someone who accompanies the golfer and didn't see the ball either.

    —JOE FRANCIS

camping: nature's way of promoting the motel business.

    —DAVE BARRY

cannibal: a guy who goes into a restaurant and orders the waiter.

— JACK BENNY

celebrity: a person who works hard all his life to become known, then wears dark glasses to avoid being recognized.

— FRED ALLEN

chess: the piece movement.

— GEORGE CARLIN

chic: knowing which fingers to put in your mouth when you whistle for the waiter.

— MILTON BERLE

children: nature's very own form of birth control.

— DAVE BARRY

Christian: a man who feels
Repentance on Sunday
For what he did on Saturday
And is going to do on Monday.
—THOMAS R. YBARRA

chrysanthemum: a flower which, by any other name, would be much easier to spell.
—WILLIAM JOHNSON

clone: a cell mate.
—ANGIE PAPADAKIS

college: a place to keep warm between high school and an early marriage.
—GEORGE GOBEL

committee: a group of people who individually can do nothing but as a group decide that nothing can be done.
—FRED ALLEN

computer: a high-tech machine that enable first-graders to make their parents feel like morons.

—JOYCE ARMOR

concentration: the ability to do your son's homework while he is watching television.

—TERRY MCCORMICK

concert: on-stage talent playing to a chorus of coughs.

—RICK BAYAN

confidence: that quiet assured feeling you have before you fall flat on your face.

—LEONARD BINDER

connoisseur: someone who can sip a glass of wine and tell you not only what year it was bottled, but who jumped on the grapes.

—STANLEY DAVIS

conscience: what hurts when all your other parts feel so good.
—STEVEN WRIGHT

consultant: a jobless person who shows executives how to work.
—RICK BAYAN

contract: an agreement that is binding only on the weaker party.
—FREDERICK SAWYER

converted cannibal: one who, on Friday, eats only fishermen.
—EMILY LOTNEY

cost-of-living index: a list of numbers which proves that high prices are not expensive.
—RICHARD WEISS

cotton balls: the final stage of beer nuts.
—GEORGE CARLIN

criminal: a person with predatory instincts who has not sufficient capital to form a corporation.

—HOWARD SCOTT

cult film: a movie seen about 50 times by about that many people.

—RICK BAYAN

culture: what your butcher would have if he were a surgeon.

—MARY PETTIBONE POOLE

cynic: just a man who found out when he was about 10 that there wasn't any Santa Claus, and he's still upset.

—JAMES GOULD COZZENS

D

dancing: a wonderful training for girls; it's the first way you learn to guess what a man is going to do before he does it.

—CHRISTOPHER MORLEY

darling: the popular form of address used in speaking to a member of the opposite sex whose name you cannot at the moment recall.

—OLIVER HERFORD

day after tomorrow: the third day of the rest of your life.

—GEORGE CARLIN

democracy: an institution in which the whole is equal to the scum of the parts.

—KEITH PRESTON

diamond: a lump of coal with a migraine.

—L.P. WHITNEY

diplomat: a person who can tell you to go to hell in such a way that you actually look forward to the trip.

—CASKIE STINNETT

doorman: a genius who can open the door of your car with one hand, help you in with the other, and still have one left for the tip.

—DOROTHY KILGALLEN

double feature: a show that enables you to sit through a picture you don't care to see, so you can see one you don't like.

—HENRY MORGAN

draft: white people sending black people to fight yellow people to protect the country they stole from red people.

—GEROME RAGNI
AND JAMES RADO

drama critic: a person who surprises the playwright by informing him what he meant.

—WILSON MIZNER

E

easy: an adjective used to describe a woman who has the sexual morals of a man.
—NANCY LINN-DESMOND

ecologist: someone who writes a 1,000-page book asking where have all the trees gone.
—JOEL ROTHMAN

economics: an entire scientific discipline of not knowing what you're talking about.
—P.J. O'ROURKE

economist: an expert who will know tomorrow why the things he predicted yesterday didn't happen today.
—EVAN ESAR

ecstasy: the feeling you feel when you feel you are going to feel a feeling you never felt before.
—LARRY WILDE

editor: a person who knows precisely what he wants but isn't quite sure.

—WALTER DAVENPORT

efficiency expert: a guy who puts unbreakable glass on all the fire alarms.

—MILTON BERLE

electricity: just organized lightning.

—GEORGE CARLIN

elephant: a mouse built to government specifications.

—ROBERT A. HEINLEIN

endless loop: n. see loop, endless.

—ISAAC ASIMOV

environmentalist: someone concerned with the influence of affluence.

—JOEL ROTHMAN

equestrians: just pedestrians with a stable influence.

  —LINDA WILLIAMS

erotica: stuff that's meant to be read with one hand.

  —CARL MANZ

escargot: French for "fat crawling bag of phlegm."

  —DAVE BARRY

eternity: the second hour of Trivial Pursuit.

  —MILTON BERLE

euthanasia: the art of persuading elderly loaded relatives to bring their wills into effect.

  —RICK BAYAN

experience: what you get when you don't get what you want.

  —DON STANFORD

expert: a lecturer from out of town, with slides.

—JIM BAUMGARTEN

F

factorial: someone's attempt to make math look exciting.

—STEVEN WRIGHT

family vacation: one where you arrive with five bags, four kids and seven I-thought-you-packed-its.

—IVERN BALL

fanatic: a man who does what he thinks the Lord would do, if He knew the facts of the case.

—FINLEY PETER DUNNE

farm: a hunk of land on which, if you get up early enough mornings and work late enough nights, you'll make a fortune: if you strike oil on it.

— FIBBER MCGEE

farmer: a handy man with a sense of humus.

— E.B. WHITE

fidelity: not having more than one man in bed at the same time.

— FREDERIC RAPHAEL

flashlight: a great gadget for storing dead batteries.

— MILTON BERLE

forecast: a pretense of knowing what would have happened if what does happen hadn't.

— RALPH HARRIS

foreign aid: taxing poor people in rich countries for the benefit of rich people in poor countries.
> —BERNARD ROSENBERG

free enterprise: getting other people to do your work.
> —LEWIS GRIZZARD

freelance writer: a man who is paid per piece or per word or perhaps.
> —ROBERT BENCHLEY

frost bite: what you get if you cross a snowman and a vampire.
> —GAIL S. ANGEL

future tense: a reason to relax now.
> —JOSEPH LEFF

G

gambling: a way of getting nothing for something.
    —WILSON MIZNER

garage sale: selling odds to meet ends.
    —JACOB BRAUDE

garden: a thing of beauty and a job forever.
    —JOEY ADAMS

genius: an average student with a Jewish grandmother.
    —MILTON BERLE

gentleman: a man who knows how to play the accordion, but doesn't.
    —AL COHN

gigolo: a fee-male.
    —ISAAC GOLDBERG

glamour: that indefinable "something" of a girl with a large bosom.
>—LEE DANIEL QUINN

glutton: an abominable stow man.
>—SHELLY FRIEDMAN

(to) gossip: to hear something you like about someone you don't.
>—EARL WILSON

government subsidy: getting just some of your own money back.
>—DANIEL J. METZGER

gravity: a contributing factor in 73 percent of all accidents involving falling objects.
>—DAVE BARRY

guilt: the reason they put the articles in *Playboy*.
>—DENNIS MILLER

H

hair: the only one real cure for baldness.
—GENE PERRET

Hamlet: the tragedy of tackling a family problem too soon after college.
—TOM MASSON

hangover: the wrath of the grapes.
—DOROTHY PARKER

hardware: the part of the computer that can be kicked.
—JEFF PESIS

harp: a nude piano.
—TOM O'HORGAN

health: what my friends are always drinking to before they fall down.
—PHYLLIS DILLER

health club patrons: men with breasts the size of lobby furniture.
> —RICHARD JENI

hell: a pocket edition of Chicago.
> —ASHLEY MONTAGU

heredity: what a man believes in until his son begins to behave like a delinquent.
> —MORT SAHL

heroes: what a guy in a boat does.
> —EDWARD THOMPSON

highbrow: anyone who can listen to the *William Tell Overture* and not think of *The Lone Ranger*.
> —JACK PERLIS

hippie: someone who looks like Tarzan, walks like Jane and smells like Cheeta.
> —RONALD REAGAN

home: a place where part of the family waits till the rest of the family brings the car back.
—EARL WILSON

homeless musician: one without a girlfriend.
—DAVE BARRY

homeopathist: the humorist of the medical profession.
—AMBROSE BIERCE

homework: something teenagers do during commercials.
—BRENDA DAVIDSON

honest executive: one who shares the credit with the person who did all the work.
—E.C. MCKENZIE

honesty: the best policy unless you are a crook.
—WINSTON GROOM

honeymoon: a short period of doting between dating and debting.
　　—ROY BANDY

hors d'oeuvre: a ham sandwich cut into 40 pieces.
　　—JACK BENNY

humility: a virtue when you have no other.
　　—EDWARD ABBEY

hymen: a greeting to male companions.
　　—MIKE LEIWIG

hypocrite: a person who: but who isn't?
　　—DON MARQUIS

I

icicles: water with a stiff upper drip.
　　　—ANN PFEIFFER

infinity: nature's way of putting things off.
　　　—DON ADDIS

imitation: the sincerest form of flattery, except when you yawn.
　　　—EVAN ESAR

incense: holy smoke.
　　　—DONNA EAKER

infant prodigy: a small child with highly imaginative parents.
　　　—R.H. CREESE

insinuate: Adam and Eve's least favorite word.
　　　—JOHNNY HART

insurance: what you pay now so when you're dead you'll have nothing to worry about.
—JOSEPH ROSENBLOOM

intuition: what leads a woman to contradict her husband even before he has said anything.
—LEE DANIEL QUINN

J

jazz: five guys playing different songs.
—STEVE MCGREW

jogger: a pedestrian who's going down a dark street.
—MILTON BERLE

jury: 12 persons who are to decide which party has the better lawyer.
—ROBERT FROST

justice: only frozen water.
—JAN HYDE

K

karate: a form of martial arts in which people who have had years and years of training can, using only their hands and feet, make some of the worst movies in the history of the world.
—DAVE BARRY

kiss: a thing of no use to one, but prized by two.
—ROBERT ZWICKEY

kitchenette: a narrow aisle that runs between a gas stove and a can of tomatoes.
—BOB BURNS

kleptomaniac: a person who helps himself because he can't help himself.
—HENRY MORGAN

L

lawnmower: a weapon of grass destruction.
—SANDY SIBERT

left hand: the hand that every married man in a singles bar keeps in his pocket.
—NANCY LINN-DESMOND

lesbian: any woman who doesn't like me.
—JASON LOVE

(to) lisp: to call a spade a thspade.
—OLIVER HERFORD

loiter: not now.
—LEOPOLD FECHTNER

loop, endless: n. see endless loop.
—ISAAC ASIMOV

loser: a stowaway on a kamikaze plane.
—CHARLIE MANNA

M

mad money: a psychiatrist's fee.
—LARRY WILDE

man: the only animal clever enough to build the Empire State Building and stupid enough to jump off it.
—ROBERT W. RUSSELL

man (the male): the second strongest sex in the world.
—PHILIP BARRY

marketing: simply sales with a college education.
—JOHN FREUND

mashed figs: a foodstuff that only your grand-mother would eat, and only then because she couldn't find her dentures.

—BILL BRYSON

Mayflower: a small ship on which several million Pilgrims came to America in 1620.

—STEVE ALLEN

menu: a list of dishes that a restaurant has just run out of.

—ERMA BOMBECK

meow: "woof" in cat.

—GEORGE CARLIN

mine: a hole in the ground owned by a liar.

—MARK TWAIN

miracle: an event described by those to whom it was told by men who did not see it.

—ELBERT HUBBARD

mistress: something that goes between a mister and a mattress.
—JOE E. LEWIS

modern sculptor: a man who can take a rough block of stone or wood, work on it for months and make it look like a rough block of stone or wood.
—CHARLES KELLY

money: the key to financial success.
—DAVID KLEINBARD

musicals: a series of catastrophes ending with a floor show.
—OSCAR LEVANT

N

natural death: when you die without the aid of a doctor.
—MARK TWAIN

nostalgia: longing for something you couldn't stand anymore.

—FIBBER McGEE

nudity: the best contraceptive for old people.

—PHYLLIS DILLER

O

octopus: an eight-sided vagina.

—GEORGE CARLIN

Olympics: the only time you can represent America and not have to carry a gun.

—GEORGE RAVELING

omen: a sign that something will happen if nothing happens.

—AMBROSE BIERCE

opera: when a guy gets stabbed in the back and instead of bleeding he sings.
>—ED GARDNER

optimist: a fellow who believes a housefly is looking for a way to get out.
>—GEORGE JEAN NATHAN

order: what exists before you start arranging things.
>—MARTY RUBIN

organ donor: someone who looks forward to being outlived by his liver.
>—RICK BAYAN

organic: just another word for dirty fruit.
>—RUBY WAX

overwork: a dangerous disorder affecting high public functionaries who want to go fishing.
>—AMBROSE BIERCE

P

parakeet: a keet that takes care of you until the real keet arrives.

—GEORGE CARLIN

paranoid-schizophrenic: someone who always thinks he is following himself.

—GENE PERRET

patience: what parents have when there are witnesses.

—FRANKLIN P. JONES

pedestrian: a fella who ignores his wife when she tells him they need two cars.

—ROBERT ORBEN

peeping Tom: a guy who is too lazy to go to the beach.

—HENNY YOUNGMAN

perfect lover: one who turns into a pizza at 4 A.M.
> —CHARLES PIERCE

petition: a list of people who didn't have the courage to say no.
> —EVAN ESAR

philanthropist: one who gives away what he should give back.
> —JOEY ADAMS

philistine: what a German bartender does.
> —ROBERT E. LEWIS

potato: an Irish avocado.
> —FRED ALLEN

P.R. man: a press agent with a manicure.
> —ALAN GORDON

psychology: the science that tells you what you already know, in words you can't understand.

—JOEY ADAMS

puck: a hard rubber disk that hockey players strike when they can't hit one another.

—JIMMY CANNON

Q

quandary: a camel with four humps.

—DIANE REAMY CAPEWELL

quantum particles: the dreams that stuff is made of.

—DAVID MOSER

R

real estate agents: God's curse on mankind when locusts are out of season.

—LEWIS GRIZZARD

reality: a crutch for people who can't cope with drugs.

—JANE WAGNER

real man: someone who can ski through an avalanche, and still manage not to spill any beer.

—BRUCE FEIRSTEIN

rectal exam: that part of the physical examination that illustrates the true meaning of the Yuletide maxim, "It is better to give than to receive."

—HOWARD BENNETT

redundancy: an air-bag in a politician's car.

—LARRY HAGMAN

refrigerator: a place where you store leftovers until they're old enough to throw out.
—AL BOLISKA

repartee: what a person thinks of after he becomes a departee.
—DAN BENNETT

recession: what the government calls a depression that spares the rich.
—RICK BAYAN

retirement: twice as much husband for half as much money.
—BETTE MIDLER

rock journalism: people who can't write, interviewing people who can't talk for people who can't read.
—FRANK ZAPPA

rubberneck: what you do to relax your wife.
—EDWARD THOMPSON

S

sadist: someone who is nice to masochists.
—VINCENT MCHUGH

Santa: Satan spelled inside out.
—GEORGE CARLIN

school bus driver: someone who thought he liked children.
—JOHN ROONEY

scout troop: 12 little kids dressed like schmucks following a big schmuck dressed like a kid.
—JACK BENNY

seaweed: something you don't want your neighbors to do when they look in your garden.
—ART LINKLETTER

secure: safe from attack by a hacker under six.
　　—STEPHEN MANES

self-delusion: pulling in your stomach when you step on the scales.
　　—PAUL SWEENEY

senile: what elderly tourists do in Egypt.
　　—TIM BRUENING

September: the month when a lot of people discover what a good time the moths had while they were on vacation.
　　—O.A. BATTISTA

septic tank: poo keeper.
　　—CHARLES G. WAUGH

seriousness: stupidity sent to college.
　　—P.J. O'ROURKE

skiing: combines outdoor fun with knocking down trees with your face.

—DAVE BARRY

snobs: people that talk as if they had begotten their own ancestors.

—HERBERT AGAR

spare ribs: what everybody else has except Adam.

—JOHNNY HART

sperm bank: only a place whose come has time.

—MILTON BERLE

spinster: an unlusted number.

—LEE DANIEL QUINN

starlet: the name for any woman under 30 not actively employed in a brothel.

—BEN HECHT

status symbol: anything you can't afford, but did.
>—HAROLD COFFIN

stick: a boomerang that doesn't work.
>—BILL KIRCHENBAUER

stockbroker: someone who invests other people's money until it's all gone.
>—WOODY ALLEN

stress: your body's way of saying you haven't worked enough unpaid overtime.
>—SCOTT ADAMS

strip teaser: a busy body.
>—JOEY ADAMS

suburbia: where the developer bulldozes out the trees, then names the streets after them.
>—BILL VAUGHAN

suicide blonde: a blonde dyed by her own hand.

—SAUL BELLOW

successful doctor: one who can keep his patients alive long enough for nature to heal them.

—DOC BLAKELY

successful parent: one who raises a child who grows up and is able to pay for their own psychoanalysis.

—NORA EPHRON

supermarket: a place where you can find anything...except your children.

—LEOPOLD FECHTNER

swimming pools: what children often confuse with a restroom.

—JOYCE ARMOR

synonym: a word you use when you can't spell the word you first thought of.
— BURT BACHARACH

syntax: all the money collected at the church from sinners.
— DOUGLAS HELSEL

T

tact: the ability to tell a man he's open-minded when he has a hole in his head.
— F.G. KERNAN

talkative woman: one who does talk as much as a man.
— CHERIS KRAMARAE

taxi: a vehicle that always seems to dissolve in the rain.
— DAN BENNETT

teenagers: God's punishment for having sex.
—PATRICK MURRAY

thesaurus: a dinosaur with a highly developed vocabulary.
—NICK SIEGLER

toastmaster: a man who eats a meal he doesn't want so he can get up and tell a lot of stories he doesn't remember to people who've already heard them.
—GEORGE JESSEL

toe: a part of the foot used to find furniture in the dark.
—RILLA MAY

topless bar: a place where you can always find a friendly face, and nobody watching it.
—JOEY ADAMS

toupee: top secret.

> —ROBERT MYERS

tourist: someone who goes 3,000 miles to get a picture of himself in front of his car.

> —ROBERT BENCHLEY

traveling: the process of journeying thousands of miles away from people to avoid them, and then sending them a card saying, "Wishing you were here."

> —E.C. MCKENZIE

tumor: an extra pair.

> —MIKE MCKINLEY

U

ubermensch: a drunken German, with a lisp.

> —LAURIE A. MURRAY

undercook: where they caught the waitress in the storeroom.

—KEN PINKHAM

university: a collection of mutually repellent individuals held together only by a common interest in parking.

—GEORGE F. WILL

upper crust: a bunch of crumbs held together by dough.

—JOSEPH A. THOMAS

urinal: the one place where all men are peers.

—RICK BAYAN

urine: opposite of you're out.

—MIKE MCKINLEY

user: the word computer professionals use when they mean "idiot."

—DAVE BARRY

V

vacation: what you take when you can no longer take what you've been taking.

—EARL WILSON

vegetarian: the Indian word for "lousy hunter."

—JEFF GARZIK

very close family: one with relations who have relations.

—CYNTHIA MACGREGOR

virginity: a big issue about a little issue.

—MILTON BERLE

voluptuous woman: one who has curves in places where some girls don't even have places.

—HENNY YOUNGMAN

voting: a process of standing in line to decide which party will waste your money.

—BABE WEBSTER

W

weaker sex: the kind you have after the kids have worn you out.

—JOHN HENRY

wealth: any income that is at least 100 dollars a year more than the income of one's wife's sister's husband.

—H.L. MENCKEN

weapon: a device for making your enemy change his mind.

—LOIS MCMASTER BUJOLD

wheel: man's greatest invention until he got behind it.

—BILL IRELAND

whodunit: none of the kids that live in your house.

—JOHN HENRY

widower: the only man who can make more money than his wife can spend.

—O.A. BATTISTA

wife: a person who can look in a drawer and find her husband's socks that aren't there.

—DAN BENNETT

woman's movie: one where the woman commits adultery all through the picture, and, at the end, her husband begs her to forgive him.

—OSCAR LEVANT

X

Xerox: a trademark for a photocopying device that can make rapid reproductions of human error, perfectly.

—MERLE L. MEACHAM

X-ray: inside information.

—HAL STEBBINS

Y

yak: a lovely long-haired animal, like a cow on the way to the opera.

—PAUL THEROUX

young: an adjective used by men to describe a woman who is under 18 or a man who is under 80.

—NANCY LINN-DESMOND

Z

zebra: what ze French women wear.
—LEOPOLD FECHTNER

Zen martini: a martini with no vermouth at all. And no gin, either.
—P.J. O'ROURKE

zig zag: the shortest distance between two bars.
—L.L. LEVINSON

zoo: the place where your child asks loud questions about the private parts of large mammals.
—JOYCE ARMOR

INDEX